W9-AYI-377

SOUTH CAROLINA

Janice Parker

AV² provides enriched content that supplements and complements this book. Weigl's AV² books strive to create inspired learning and engage young minds in a total learning experience.

Your AV² Media Enhanced books come alive with...

Audio
Listen to sections of the book read aloud.

Video
Watch informative video clips.

Embedded Weblinks
Gain additional information for research.

Try This!
Complete activities and hands-on experiments.

Key Words
Study vocabulary, and complete a matching word activity.

Quizzes
Test your knowledge.

Slide Show
View images and captions, and prepare a presentation.

... and much, much more!

Go to **www.av2books.com**, and enter this book's unique code.

BOOK CODE

V289962

AV² by Weigl brings you media enhanced books that support active learning.

Published by AV² by Weigl
350 5th Avenue, 59th Floor
New York, NY 10118
Website: www.av2books.com

Library of Congress Cataloging-in-Publication Data
Names: Parker, Janice, author.
Title: South Carolina : the Palmetto State / Janice Parker.
Description: New York, NY : AV2 by Weigl, [2016] | Series: Discover America |
  Includes index.
Identifiers: LCCN 2015048044 (print) | LCCN 2015048336 (ebook) | ISBN
  9781489649386 (hard cover : alk. paper) | ISBN 9781489649393 (soft cover :
  alk. paper) | ISBN 9781489649409 (Multi-User eBook)
Subjects: LCSH: South Carolina--Juvenile literature.
Classification: LCC F269.3 .P37 2016 (print) | LCC F269.3 (ebook) | DDC 975.7--dc23
LC record available at http://lccn.loc.gov/2015048044

Printed in the United States of America, in Brainerd, MInnesota
1 2 3 4 5 6 7 8 9 20 19 18 17 16

082016
210716

Project Coordinator Heather Kissock
Art Director Terry Paulhus

Photo Credits
Every reasonable effort has been made to trace ownership and to obtain permission to reprint copyright material. The publisher would be pleased to have any errors or omissions brought to their attention so that they may be corrected in subsequent printings. The publisher acknowledges Getty Images, iStock Images, Shutterstock, and Alamy as its primary image suppliers for this title.

SOUTH CAROLINA

Contents

STATE TREE
Cabbage Palmetto

STATE ANIMAL
White-tailed Deer

STATE FLAG
South Carolina

STATE BIRD
Carolina Wren

STATE FLOWER
Yellow Jasmine

STATE SEAL
South Carolina

Nicknames
The Palmetto State

Song
"Carolina," words by Henry Timrod and music by Anne Custis Burgess, and "South Carolina on My Mind," words and music by Hank Martin and Buzz Arledge

Entered the Union
May 23, 1788, as the 8th state

Motto
Animis Opibusque Parati (Prepared in Mind and Resources) and *Dum Spiro Spero* (While I Breathe, I Hope)

Population
(2010 Census) 4,625,364
Ranked 24th state

Capital
Columbia

Discover South Carolina

South Carolina is a state to celebrate, and South Carolinians have the festivals to prove it. South Carolina's food is celebrated with the Lowcountry Shrimp Festival, the Peanut Party in Pelion, and the Watermelon Festival in Hampton. Residents rejoice in the natural beauty of their state with festivals for roses as well as irises, and the South Carolina Festival of Flowers in Greenwood. They honor their history by preserving numerous American Revolutionary War and Civil War battlefields, and South Carolinians stage dramatic re-creations of major Civil War battles and other battles.

The smallest state in the Deep South, South Carolina has a varied landscape and a warm climate. With its friendly residents and natural beauty, including mountains and seashores, the state also boasts a booming tourist industry. Hilton Head, an island off the coast of South Carolina, attracts more than 2 million tourists every year. The state has more than 24 championship golf courses. Visitors also enjoy the quiet beauty of nature preserves, such as Sea Pines Forest Preserve and Audubon-Newhall Preserve.

Once based primarily on agriculture, the economy of South Carolina has gradually moved toward an industrial-based economy. Today, manufacturing is one of the most significant industries in South Carolina. North Charleston is home to a Boeing assembly plant, Greenville is home to GE's wind energy engineering site, and Duncan, North Carolina is a hub for solar panel manufacturing and sales.

The Land

South Carolina's nickname, **the Palmetto State**, comes from the distinctive tree that grows along the state's coast.

South Carolina's Atlantic coastline is approximately **187 miles long**, but if all the bays, inlets, and islands are included, the state has **2,876 miles** of coastline.

Beginnings

The first people arrived in the area of South Carolina about 15,000 years ago. They were hunters and used simple tools. Eventually, these prehistoric people developed farming technology. Evidence of pottery and simple farming exists from about 10,000 years ago. By the time Europeans arrived, there were about 29 Native American groups living in the region.

British settlers established a colony in South Carolina in the late 1600s. Many of the colonists owned **plantations** and grew crops such as rice and cotton. They used slaves from Africa to work in the fields.

During the mid-1800s, a dispute between the northern and southern states arose over the issue of state's rights and whether or not slavery should be allowed to continue. While much of the North opposed slavery, the South wanted to keep its slaves and plantation culture. On December 20, 1860, South Carolina became the first state to **secede** from the United States, or the Union. It became part of the Confederate States of America.

The Civil War began on April 12, 1861, when Confederate troops fired upon Fort Sumter in Charleston Harbor. During the war, South Carolina's coast was the site of much fighting. After the Confederacy was defeated by the United States, South Carolina was readmitted to the Union. The state began to rebuild its economy without slavery. New industries, such as textiles, helped pave the way to a brighter future.

After the Civil War, textiles became an important industry for South Carolina. By 1910, almost 150 mills employed 45,000 workers.

Where is
SOUTH CAROLINA?

South Carolina is shaped like a triangle. The state is bordered by North Carolina to the north and northeast, Georgia to the west and southwest, and the Atlantic Ocean to the east and southeast. South Carolina's land area of 30,109 square miles makes it the 11th smallest state in the nation.

United States Map

South Carolina

Alaska   Hawai'i

MAP LEGEND
- ■ South Carolina
- ☆ Capital City
- ◢ Huntington Beach State Park
- ▼ Port Royal
- ― Savannah River
- □ Bordering States
- □ Water

GEORGIA

1 Columbia

Named for the naval explorer Christopher Columbus, Columbia was chosen to be the capital in 1786 because it was near the center of the state. Although two-thirds of Columbia was burned to the ground during the Civil War, it still contains historic homes and the First Baptist Church, where South Carolinians decided to secede from the Union.

2 Port Royal

Sitting at the head of Port Royal Sound is one of South Carolina's Sea Islands, Port Royal. The island was named by French naval officer Jean Ribaut, who led an expedition to the area in the sixteenth century. Throughout the American Revolutionary War and Civil War, Port Royal was occupied by both sides in each conflict.

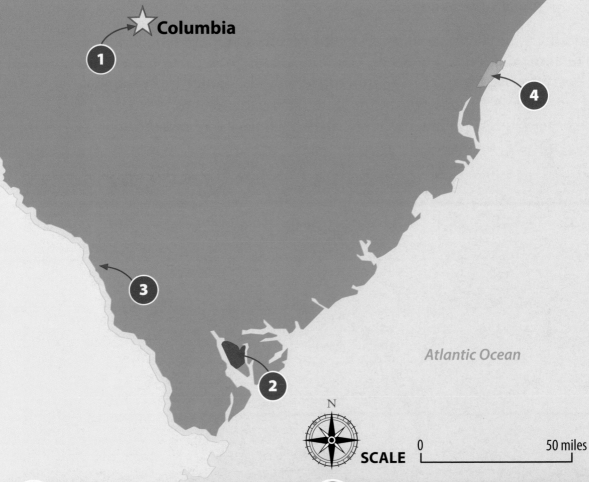

NORTH CAROLINA

SOUTH CAROLINA

★ Columbia

1

4

3

2

Atlantic Ocean

N

SCALE

0   50 miles

---

3 **Savannah River**

The Savannah River forms South Carolina's border with Georgia. The river is important for naval navigation and creating power. Both hydroelectric and nuclear power are generated at the plant near Aiken. Spanish explorers called the river *Rio Dulce*, meaning "Sweet River," and its Native American name was *Isondega*, meaning "Blue Water."

4 **Huntington Beach State Park**

The Huntington Beach State Park was created by Archer and Anna Hyatt Huntington. More than 300 bird species live in the park, making it one of the best birdwatching spots in South Carolina. The park also includes the Moorish-style mansion Atalaya of the Huntingtons, which hosts art festivals.

Land Features

South Carolina has three distinct land regions. The low-lying Atlantic Coastal Plain in the southern and eastern parts of the state is mainly flat. Farther inland is the Piedmont, a plateau with rolling hills that covers about one-third of the state. The Blue Ridge region is a tiny area in the northwestern portion of the state. It is dominated by the Blue Ridge Mountains.

South Carolina also includes 13 major islands and many smaller ones. The three main rivers of South Carolina are the Santee, Savannah, and Great Pee Dee Rivers. At 143 miles in length, the Santee is the longest river that falls entirely within the state. There are no large natural lakes in South Carolina, but many artificial ones have been created by damming the major rivers.

Barrier Islands

Barrier islands lie off South Carolina's eastern coast. These long islands are typically composed of sand carried by ocean waves. Beaches, dunes, swampy areas, and different kinds of plants cover the islands.

Subtropical Forest

Moss-draped live oaks, magnolia trees, loblolly pines, holly trees, southern red cedars, and wild palmettos are just a few of the trees that thrive in the subtropical forests of South Carolina.

ACE Basin

The ACE Basin, named after the Ashepoo, Combahee, and Edistor Rivers, is a protected area of marshes, wetlands, forests, and rivers. Once used for growing rice, the area gradually became hunting land. A combination of government and private funding has helped preserve much of the area in its natural state.

Blue Ridge Mountains

Part of the Appalachian Mountain chain, the Blue Ridge Mountains form a narrow ridge. This ridge ranges from 5 to 65 miles wide and from 2,000 to 4,000 feet high. The mountains get their name from the blue haze that often wraps around the peaks.

Climate

South Carolina has a subtropical climate with hot, humid summers and mild winters. Average January temperatures in South Carolina range from about 40° to 50° Fahrenheit. In July, most of the state has an average temperature of about 80°F, except in the mountains, where temperatures average around 70°F.

South Carolina can see some extreme weather. Summer usually brings the most rainfall, along with thunderstorms. An average of 10 tornadoes touch down in South Carolina every year, usually in spring. Hurricanes sometimes hit coastal areas.

Average Annual Precipitation Across South Carolina

Cities in various parts of South Carolina typically receive somewhat different amounts of rainfall over the course of a year, but the differences are not very large. What might account for the relative uniformity of rainfall across the state?

LEGEND

Average Annual Precipitation (in inches) 1961–1990

200 – 100.1

100 – 25.1

25 – 5 and less

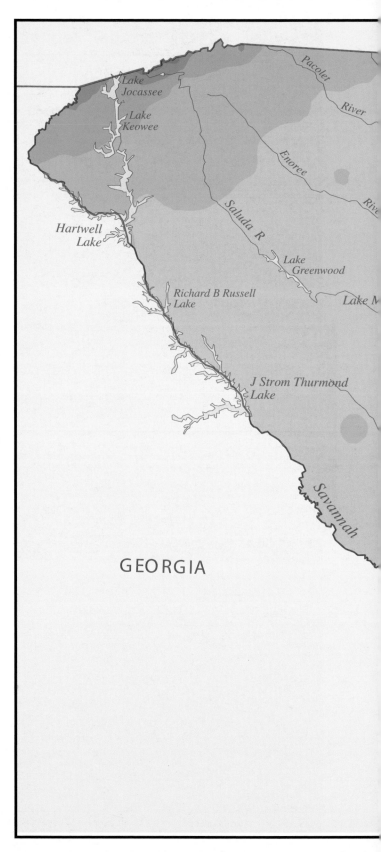

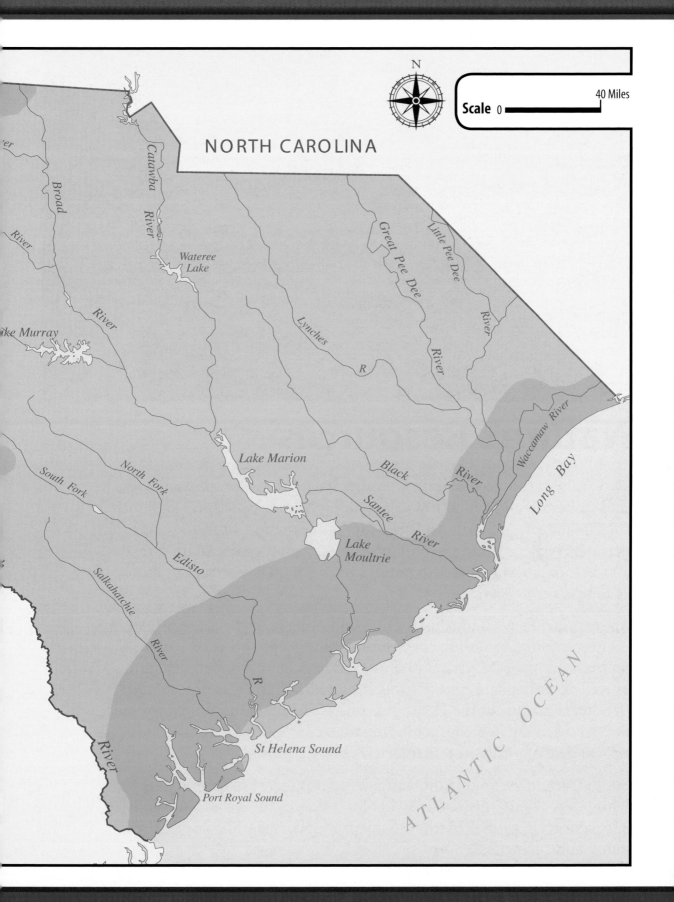

NORTH CAROLINA

N

Scale 0 ▬▬▬▬ 40 Miles

River

Broad

River

Catawba River

Wateree Lake

Lake Murray

River

Lynches

R

Great Pee Dee

Little Pee Dee

River

River

Waccamaw River

Long Bay

South Fork

North Fork

Lake Marion

Black

River

Santee

River

Edisto

Lake Moultrie

Salkahatchie

River

R

River

St Helena Sound

Port Royal Sound

ATLANTIC OCEAN

Much of South Carolina's mining industry is centered around construction materials, such as granite. Crushed granite can be used to make concrete and asphalt for roads.

Nature's Resources

Natural resources in South Carolina include vast forests, rich soils, minerals, and a plentiful water supply. About two-thirds of South Carolina is forested. Almost three-fourths of the forests in the state are privately owned. South Carolina's beaches, swamps, mountain forests, and nature preserves are also natural resources. They attract millions of tourists every year.

Many minerals used in construction and other industries are mined in South Carolina, including clay, granite, limestone, and vermiculite. A lightweight material, vermiculite is used in potting soil and insulation, as well as to incubate eggs or grow fungi. Limestone was first mined in South Carolina in the 1820s. It is one of the main ingredients of portland cement, which is a binding material. South Carolina produces a great deal of portland cement each year.

South Carolina is among the nation's top producers of kaolin, a soft, white clay. There were about 30 kaolin mines in the state in the early 21st century. Kaolin is used in many products, including paper, tires, paint, and cosmetics.

The Ashley River Road at the Magnolia Plantation and Gardens is a historic tourist site, offering visitors a look at South Carolina's swamps.

In South Carolina's forestry industry, hardwoods, such as oak, are harvested for lumber while softwoods, such as pine, are used for pulp and paper products.

Vegetation

Considering its small size, South Carolina has a large variety of plants. Loblolly and longleaf pine trees are common throughout the state's forests. Other trees include oak, cypress, magnolia, elm, sycamore, and tupelo. White pine and hemlock grow throughout the woodlands of the Pine Ridge. In the Piedmont area, vast forests of loblolly pines have replaced worn-out farmland.

Flowering shrubs and wildflowers grow throughout the state, including flowering dogwood and yellow jessamine, or jasmine. Mountain laurel and various types of rhododendron thrive in the mountain regions. Cattails and bulrushes sway in the freshwater marshes along the coast, while cordgrass, black rushes, glasswort, and sea ox-eye flourish in the saltwater marshes. The state tree, the cabbage palmetto, also grows along the coast.

Cabbage Palmetto

An evergreen palm tree, the cabbage palmetto can grow as tall as 33 feet. Its leaves can be as large as 3 feet across. Raccoons, robins, and other birds feed on the tree's fruit. People use its big leaf bud in salads, pickles, and relishes.

Venus Flytrap

Each leaf of this rare plant is hinged at the middle. This feature allows it to snap shut around any insect or spider that lands on it. The plant's sap then digests its prey.

Kudzu

Kudzu can grow up to 1 foot every day. People used to plant it to control **erosion**. Now it has become a pest, covering and killing plants by blocking the sunlight they need to grow.

Sea Oats

These grasses thrive in sandy areas and can grow up to 6 feet tall. They trap windblown sand that eventually forms into dunes. Sea oats also tolerate salt water, making them excellent beach cover for protecting coastlines from erosion.

Wildlife

Common wild animals in the state include the white-tailed deer, beavers, and squirrels. Hundreds of species of birds have been spotted in South Carolina. Hawks, owls, wild turkeys, and bald eagles live in the state. Other native birds include the swallow, Baltimore oriole, and pelican. South Carolina's coast is part of the Atlantic Flyway, a north-south route used by many species of birds during their annual migration.

Turtles, lizards, salamanders, frogs, and toads can be found in South Carolina's swamps. Dolphins swim offshore. The largest reptile in North America is the American alligator. It lives in the lakes, streams, and swamps of the state's Atlantic Coastal Plain. The American alligator can be as long as 20 feet. It is black with bands of yellow that fade with age. This alligator can be dangerous to humans.

Wild Turkey

A wild turkey's head is normally red but turns white and bright blue when it is excited. A wattle hangs from its throat. Male turkeys can weigh up to 22 pounds, while females are much smaller.

Loggerhead Turtle

The shell of an adult loggerhead turtle can grow to 3 or 4 feet long. These sea turtles have huge jaws to crush clamshells. They appear on land only to lay their eggs in the sand.

Bottlenose Dolphin

Graceful, friendly, and intelligent, bottlenose dolphins communicate with clicks, squeals, and whistles. Speedy swimmers, these toothed whales can reach almost 18 miles per hour in short bursts.

White-tailed Deer

The white-tailed deer is the oldest living species of deer in the world. Adult deer coats are reddish brown in summer and grayish brown in winter. Fawns, or baby deer, are spotted. This coloring helps them blend in with the forest floor to hide from predators.

Economy

Myrtle Beach

Amusement parks are among the many attractions of Myrtle Beach. Ferris wheels carry riders to great heights, allowing them to look over the parks and cities below. Myrtle Beach Pavilion Amusement Park boasts the state's largest wooden roller coaster and an arcade along the ocean.

Tourism

Known for its warm climate, lush mountains, long coastline, and friendly people, South Carolina is a popular tourist destination. In fact, an average of 28.5 million people traveled to South Carolina each year during the late 2000s. Many came to explore the Grand Strand area, which enjoys more than 200 sunny days each year. Myrtle Beach is located along the Grand Strand.

Many other attractions draw visitors to the state. South Carolina's lakes attract families for fishing, waterskiing, kayaking, and canoeing. Some people visit the mountains to hike and explore nature. Others ride the roller coasters at the state's many amusement parks. History buffs travel to Charleston, where they can tour buildings from the colonial period. Charleston also has many museums, including the Confederate Museum, which displays Confederate army uniforms and equipment.

Fort Sumter

Fort Sumter was built on an artificial island in Charleston's harbor. Enduring four years of cannon fire during the Civil War, much of the fort was completely destroyed. Today, the Fort Sumter National Monument includes a partially rebuilt fort and a museum with historical displays.

Hilton Head

While serious golfers may flock to Hilton Head for the championship courses, miniature golf attracts families and players of all ages. Visitors can also explore charming small towns or go shell hunting on the island's gorgeous beaches.

Magnolia Plantation and Gardens

The Magnolia Plantation and Gardens is on the site of a large farm that was founded in Charleston in 1676. It features the Barbados Tropical Garden, the oldest public garden in the United States.

South Carolina is famous for its peaches, which grow in the upper Piedmont and midland regions.

Primary Industries

Agriculture was the backbone of South Carolina's economy through the early 1900s. Although agriculture is still important to the state, many more South Carolinians now work in service and manufacturing industries. Manufacturing focuses on textiles, industrial machinery, and chemicals.

One of the state's leading agricultural products is broiler chickens, which are chickens raised for eating, not for producing eggs. Turkeys, cattle, cotton, soybeans, tomatoes, and peanuts are also important agricultural products. South Carolina is one of the largest producers in the nation of peaches and flue-cured tobacco. Flue-cured tobacco is dried by artificial heat rather than hung to air-dry. Tobacco, grown primarily in the Pee Dee region, accounts for nearly one-fourth of all income earned from crops in South Carolina.

Much of South Carolina is forested, almost 13 million acres. Pine, oaks, and other hardwood trees make up much of the forestland. The state produces about $1 billion in forest products, including paper products and wood for construction.

While it was in use from 1988 to 1990, South Carolina's **Ridgeway gold mine** was the only mine producing gold east of the Mississippi River.

More than **54,000 acres** of **tobacco** are harvested each year in South Carolina.

Value of Goods and Services
(in Millions of Dollars)

South Carolina once relied on agriculture to support its economy. However, tourism has become one of the fastest-growing sources of income in the state. What industries thrive to a large extent by meeting the needs of tourists?

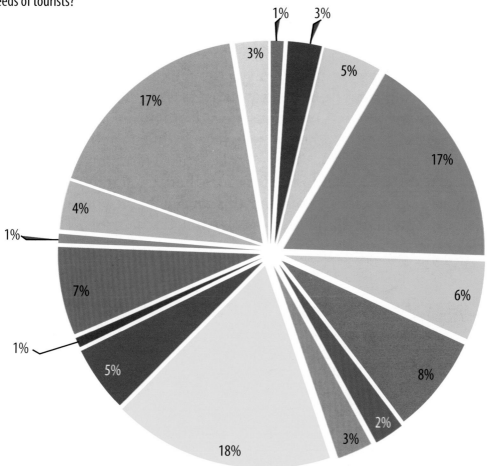

● Agriculture, forestry, fishing, & mining $1,739	● Professional, Scientific, & Technical Services .. $9,161
● Utilities $4,643	● Education $1,330
● Construction $8,236	● Health Care & Social Assistance $12,272
● Manufacturing $29,792	● Arts, Entertainment, & Recreation $1,284
● Wholesale Trade $10,977	● Accommodation & Food Services $6,843
● Retail Trade $13,582	● Government $29,872
● Transportation & Warehousing $4,217	● Other Services $4,597
● Information $4,904	*less than 1%
● Finance, Insurance, & Real Estate $30,752	

Goods and Services

Chemicals are the leading manufactured products in South Carolina. The main products in this category include plastic resins, dyes, and medicines. The major centers for chemical production are the cities of Greenville, Spartanburg, Columbia, and Aiken.

The production of textiles, or cloth, fibers, and yarn, has a long and important economic history in the state. Even though the majority of textile-manufacturing facilities were moved overseas in the late twentieth century, many South Carolinians are still employed by textile companies. Milliken & Company, which is headquartered in Spartanburg, is one of the nation's largest textile firms. The company has a large textile research center and holds more than 2,300 **patents** in the United States alone. Mount Vernon Mills, Inc., a textile company based in Mauldin, is another of the country's leading textile firms. The company dates back to the 1840s.

South Carolina has grown cotton for centuries. While less important today, South Carolina's textile industry still relies on the cotton grown in the state.

Nearly 10 percent of South Carolina's workforce is employed in the tourism industry. In addition to tourism, service industries in the state employing workers include government, retail and wholesale businesses, and health-care facilities. Financial services and firms providing other business services also service and employ many.

South Carolina has numerous facilities for higher education. The University of South Carolina, which was chartered in 1801, educates more than 32,000 students on its eight campuses. It offers about 320 degree programs for its students.

Charleston is considered one of the most popular tourist destinations in the country. Visitors come to the city to experience the pre-Civil War South.

The University of South Carolina is based in Columbia and has seven satellite campuses throughout the state.

History

The Catawba were considered one of the strongest Siouan cultures in the South. They are still honored today in what is their traditional homeland, the northern regions of South Carolina.

Native Americans

About 900 years ago, a group called the Mound Builders flourished in the area that is now South Carolina. The Mound Builders were known for building great mounds of earth, which were used as burial grounds or ceremony sites. The Santee Indian Mound is one of the last remaining mounds in the state, and is the largest mound found on the coastal plain.

By the 1600s, about 30 different groups of Native Americans lived in the South Carolina region. They had a total population of about 15,000. Two groups that lived in the northern and western parts of the region were the Cherokee and the Catawba. Unlike many other groups in the Southeast who spoke Muskogean languages, the Cherokees spoke an Iroquoian language. They lived in villages with homes made from small trees, mud, and bark.

The Catawbas spoke a Siouan language and were known for their tradition of making pottery. Early Catawba potters worked with clay that was sometimes mixed with Spanish moss. They often rolled the clay into coils, which they then formed into bowls. The Catawbas wore clothes of deerskin, and in the winter, they added capes and leggings made of other animal skins. Their jewelry was made of shells, beads, and copper.

Today, the largest Native American group in South Carolina is the Pee Dee. The ancestors of the Pee Dees raised squash, corn, and beans, and gathered nuts, berries, and other fruits. Most Pee Dees today live in the northeast.

The Cherokee National Museum features reconstructions of traditional Cherokee summer homes to help visitors visualize what life was like for the Native American group.

Exploring the Land

In 1521, Francisco Gordillo led a Spanish expedition that explored the coast of what is now South Carolina. He stopped to trade goods with the Native Americans along the coast. When he left, he took more than 100 Native Americans with him as slaves.

Lucas Vásquez de Ayllón, another Spanish explorer, came to the area in 1526 with about 600 people. He started a colony near present-day Georgetown. The colony faced many difficulties. Illness, conflicts with the Native Americans, and bad weather forced the group to return home after just a few months.

Timeline of Settlement

European Settlements and Control

1562 French Huguenots led by Captain Jean Ribaut build a fort on Parris Island.

1526 Spanish explorer Lucas Vásquez de Ayllón tries to establish a colony, which ultimately fails due to disease and other factors.

1521 Francisco Gordillo from Spain leads an expedition that explores what is now South Carolina.

Early Exploration

1670 British lord Anthony Ashley Cooper starts a small colony at Albemarle Point, the first permanent European settlement in South Carolina. The colony later moves to what will become the site of Charleston.

1719 Carolina, consisting of present-day North and South Carolina, becomes a separate royal province ruled by the British.

In 1562, the French tried unsuccessfully to start a colony on Parris Island. Captain Jean Ribaut and a small group of French Huguenots built a fort there. The Huguenots were Protestants who left France to escape religious **persecution**. Soon after they arrived, Ribaut sailed back to France to get more men and supplies. He did not return, however, and the Huguenots soon abandoned the settlement. A few years later, a group of Spanish settlers established a colony on the island at Santa Elena. However, in 1587, the town and fort were abandoned as the Spanish withdrew from the area.

1783 After the American Revolutionary War, Great Britain formally recognizes the independence of the United States, which includes South Carolina.

1788 South Carolina becomes the 8th state on May 23.

Civil War and Reunification

1860 South Carolina secedes from the Union.

1776 South Carolina joins 12 other British colonies in declaring their independence. The colonists win two major victories against the British in South Carolina, at the Battle of Kings Mountain in 1780 and the Battle of Cowpens in 1781.

1861–1865 South Carolina fights on the side of the Confederacy in the Civil War. After four years of war, the Confederacy is defeated.

Independence and Statehood

1729 The British split the province into North and South Carolina.

1868 South Carolina is readmitted to the Union as a state.

The land in South Carolina is very fertile, making farms and plantations profitable for early settlers.

The First Settlers

In 1629, King Charles I of Great Britain granted parts of North America to Sir Robert Heath. This area included a strip of land containing what are now the states of South Carolina and North Carolina. The British did not immediately colonize the area, however.

In 1663, King Charles II granted the land to eight other British noblemen, and they sent settlers there. In 1670, nearly 150 colonists created the first permanent European settlement in what is now South Carolina. Many of the colonists had been living on the island of Barbados. They called their new settlement Charles Town. Ten years later, the settlement was moved across the river to a better location, the site of present-day Charleston.

Some 5,000 people had settled in the area by 1700. The population included some French Huguenots, who came from New England. In 1729, Carolina was split into North Carolina and South Carolina. By the following year, South Carolina was home to about 30,000 settlers, who lived mostly in or around Charles Town.

During the mid-1700s, a rivalry began between people living in two different areas of South Carolina. These areas were the Low Country, or the low-lying land of the coastal plain including Charles Town, and the Up Country, which was farther inland and higher in elevation. Low Country residents were often wealthy plantation owners. Much of their land was cultivated by Africans who were made to work as slaves. The Up Country, on the other hand, was populated by owners of small farms who did not use slaves.

Slave quarters were much rougher than the plantation owners', usually just a simple stone or wood cottage.

Drayton Hall, built in the eighteenth century, was the only plantation house on the Ashley River to survive both the American Revolutionary and Civil Wars intact.

History Makers

South Carolinians have contributed to their state, nation, and the world in many ways. Some have advocated tirelessly for the rights of African Americans, women, and children. Others have served their state and their nation as political or military leaders.

Angelina Grimke (1805–1879)

Angelina Grimke and her older sister Sarah worked tirelessly against slavery and for women's rights. Both sisters were born in Charleston but moved north to Philadelphia because of their strong antislavery beliefs. Angelina and Sarah became popular lecturers, attracting thousands to their speeches.

Mary McLeod Bethune (1875–1955)

Born near Mayesville, Bethune was one of 17 children of parents who were once slaves. In 1904, she started a school for African American girls in Florida. She developed the school into a 14-building campus with more than 400 students. Bethune advised presidents Calvin Coolidge, Herbert Hoover, and Franklin D. Roosevelt on the issues of children's health and education, and the rights of African Americans and other minorities.

James Byrnes (1879–1972)

This U.S. statesman served in all three branches of the federal government and was also active in state government. He represented South Carolina in the House of Representatives and in the Senate. After serving as a Supreme Court **justice**, Byrnes advised President Franklin Roosevelt during World War II.

Marian Wright Edelman (1939–)

Edelman founded the Children's Defense Fund. This organization seeks to reduce the abuse and neglect of children and the number of children living in poverty. Edelman was the first African American woman to become a lawyer in Mississippi.

Jesse Jackson (1941–)

A political leader, minister, and civil rights activist, Jesse Jackson began working in the civil rights movement in 1966, directing Operation Breadbasket. During the 1970s and 1980s, he expanded his focus, promoting voter registration and political activism as ways to achieve equal rights for all U.S. citizens.

Culture

For 17 days, the Spoleto Festival fills Charleston with a variety of art and entertainment. This includes opera, theater, dance, and different kinds of music.

A great number of South Carolinians have ancestors who fought in the Civil War, and they continue to celebrate this heritage today. The anniversary celebration of the historic 1863 Battle of Battery Wagner is held on Morris Island.

The People Today

According to the 2010 U.S. Census, the population of South Carolina is more than 4.6 million. More than two-thirds of the population is made up of people of European descent, and about 28 percent of the population is African American. Over the last 20 years, the number of people of Hispanic descent living in South Carolina has been increasing. Hispanic Americans now make up about 4.5 percent of the population.

Historically, South Carolina has had a mostly **rural** population. By 2010, more than half of South Carolinians lived in **urban** areas. South Carolina had a population density of 154 people per square mile. This number was significantly higher than the national average of about 87 people per square mile. The largest city in South Carolina is Columbia, with a population of just over 132,000. Charleston, the second-largest city is home to more than 130,000 people.

Over the past two decades, South Carolina's population has grown **significantly**, by more than **15 percent** between **2000** and **2010** alone.

Q What factors might draw people to this state?

State Government

South Carolina's constitution, which sets forth the way the state is governed, was adopted in 1895. This constitution has been amended extensively since the late 1960s. Like the federal government, the South Carolina government has three branches. They are the executive branch, the legislative branch, and the judicial branch.

The state governor heads the executive branch. The governor may serve two terms. The executive branch includes several other elected officials. The lieutenant governor, secretary of state, attorney general, treasurer, superintendent of education, and commissioner of agriculture are all part of the executive branch.

South Carolina's state legislature is called the General Assembly. It includes a House of Representatives with 124 members and a Senate with 46 members. The judicial branch is the state court system. The highest court is the Supreme Court.

Seating in South Carolina's House Chamber is divided by county, rather than party, as it is in many other legislatures.

Construction began on South Carolina's capitol building in 1851. Due to architect disputes, faulty materials, and the Civil War, it was not completed until 1907.

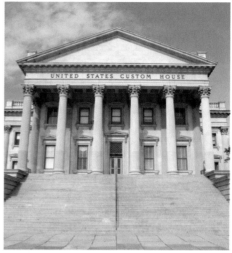

The United States Custom House in Charleston was completed in 1879. The building handles paperwork for people entering the United States from other countries.

South Carolina's state song is
"South Carolina's It for Me."

At the foot hills of the Appalachian chain,
Down through the rivers,
to the coastal plain,
There's a place that I call home,
And I'll never be alone,
Singin' this Carolina love song
I've got South Carolina on my mind
Remembering all those
sunshine Summertimes,
And the Autumns in the Smokies
when the leaves turn to gold
Touches my heart and thrills my soul
to have South Carolina on my mind,
With those clean snow-covered
mountain Wintertimes
And the white sand of the beaches
and those Carolina peaches,
I've got South Carolina on my mind.

* excerpted

The Kahal Kadosh Beth Elohim Synagogue in Charleston is the oldest continuously used Jewish synagogue in the state and one of the oldest in the nation.

Celebrating Culture

By the 1680s, people from Scotland and France were immigrating to South Carolina. The Scotch-Irish are people of Scottish origin who lived for a time in the north of Ireland. As land in Ireland grew increasingly expensive, the Scotch-Irish moved to South Carolina during the mid-1700s, drawn by the offer of free land by the colony's government. Some Scotch-Irish also came from Pennsylvania and Virginia.

The government of colonial South Carolina allowed for religious freedom. This encouraged Quakers, Baptists, Presbyterians, and Jews to immigrate to the state. By 1800, Charleston contained one of the largest Jewish populations of any city in the United States.

Many Africans were brought to South Carolina and forced to work as slaves during the 1700s and 1800s. By the late 1800s, three-fifths of the state's people were African American. However, many African Americans left South Carolina, and other areas of the Deep South, from 1916 to 1970. Better-paying jobs in factories and other businesses drew African Americans to northern urban areas.

Today, some museums in the state showcase the history and culture of African Americans in South Carolina. The Mann-Simons Cottage in Columbia houses the Museum of African-American Culture. The Avery Research Center for African American History and Culture is in Charleston. Visitors to its museum can see photographs, documents, paintings, and other items about the cultural heritage of African Americans.

The Gullah came from West Africa. They were first brought to work as slaves in the early seventeenth century. Many Gullah communities in South Carolina were located on small islands. The Gullah's unique culture includes traditional storytelling, special fish and rice dishes, and basket making and other crafts. Today, communities of Gullah live in the Charleston and Georgetown areas, as well as on Hilton Head and other islands off the South Carolina coast.

Reenactors at the Boone Hall Plantation allow visitors to experience life on a plantation in the nineteenth century.

Gullah culture is celebrated during several festivals throughout the year, where traditional folk singing is a main event.

Built in the French Quarter of Charleston, the Dock Street Theatre was originally a hotel, but converted into a theater in 1935. It was put on the National Register of Historic Places in 1973.

Arts and Entertainment

South Carolina has many notable art museums. The South Carolina State Museum in Columbia has an extensive collection of South Carolina art, as well as other exhibits on history and science. The Charleston Museum, the United States' first museum, was founded in 1773. Its goal is to preserve and exhibit the cultural and natural history of South Carolina.

South Carolina has a long history of theater. The state boasts the nation's first building designed solely for theatrical performances. In 1736, the Dock Street Theatre opened in Charleston. The theater burned down in the fire of 1740, a blaze that destroyed the city's French quarter. In 1937, the building was restored and reopened as the Dock Street Theatre. Today, more than 100,000 people attend performances there each year.

Founded in 1748, the **Charleston Library Society** is one of the **oldest libraries** in the U.S.

Colonial Life Arena is the **largest concert venue** in the state, with a seating capacity of 19,000.

Author Pat Conroy was born in Georgia but moved to South Carolina at a young age. In 1972, Conroy published a novel called *The Water Is Wide*. The National Education Association honored Conroy with an award for the book, which was later made into the film *Conrack*. Conroy's best-known novel is *The Prince of Tides*, published in 1986. The novel was made into a film starring Barbra Streisand and Nick Nolte.

Jazz trumpeter and composer Dizzy Gillespie was born in Cheraw in 1917. Along with Charlie Parker, Gillespie is considered to be one of the founders of the bebop movement in jazz. Bebop is a style of jazz based on complex **improvisation** that was developed in the 1940s.

Legendary singer and performer Eartha Kitt was born in South Carolina in 1928. She is best known for her work on Broadway. Other notable South Carolina natives include comedians Chris Rock and Aziz Ansari. Actresses Viola Davis, Mary Louise Parker, and Andie McDowell were also born in the state.

Known for her distinctive style, Eartha Kitt had many top hit songs, including the Christmas smash hit "Santa Baby."

Sports and Recreation

South Carolina's varied landscape and warm climate are perfectly suited to all types of outdoor recreation. With 47 state parks, camping and hiking are year-round activities in South Carolina. Boating, sailing, swimming, waterskiing, **parasailing**, canoeing, and kayaking are water sports that are enjoyed in the state.

South Carolina is one of the premier golfing states in the nation. There are golf courses in every region of the state. The Heritage golf tournament is held each year on Hilton Head Island.

The Clemson Tigers are among college football's best teams, with **5 undefeated seasons** and **21 conference championships**. The team has sent 194 players to the NFL.

Shoeless Joe Jackson, born in Brandon Mills, South Carolina, was one of the leading baseball players of the early twentieth century.

The Heritage Classic, now known as the RBC Heritage, has been played at Hilton head since 1969.

Steeplechase is a popular spectator sport in the state. The Carolina Cup, established in 1930, is hailed as South Carolina's largest sporting event. More than 60,000 fans come to Camden's Springdale Race Course to watch Thoroughbred horses race at 35 miles per hour over 5-foot-high fences.

The era of NASCAR speedway racing began at the Darlington Raceway on September 4, 1950. While at the raceway, people can visit the Darlington Raceway Stock Car Museum and NMPA Hall of Fame. The museum houses a large collection of historic race cars and driver memorabilia.

In 2014, jockey Darren Nagle won one of the steeplechase's top honors, the Colonial Cup, atop his horse Divine Fortune.

Although South Carolina does not have any major league professional sports teams, many South Carolinians have played professional sports. Aiken native William Perry, nicknamed "The Refrigerator," was a defensive lineman for the Chicago Bears. He was part of the team when it won the National Football League's Super Bowl in 1986. Larry Doby, who was born in Camden, became the first African American athlete to play baseball in the American League in 1947, and the second African American to play in the major leagues.

Darlington Raceway has been nicknamed "The Track Too Tough To Be Tamed" thanks to its unique egg shape, which makes the course difficult to navigate.

Get To Know
SOUTH CAROLINA

North and South Carolina are thought to be the *only* places in the world where the Venus flytrap grows in nature.

LOCATED IN SPARTANBURG, DUNCAN PARK BASEBALL STADIUM IS THE OLDEST MINOR LEAGUE STADIUM IN THE U.S

THE FIRST CLUB FOR GOLFERS IN THE UNITED STATES, THE **SOUTH CAROLINA GOLF CLUB,** WAS CREATED BY SCOTTISH SETTLERS IN CHARLESTON ON SEPTEMBER 29, 1786.

South Carolina is home to dozens of **snake** species, five of which are venomous.

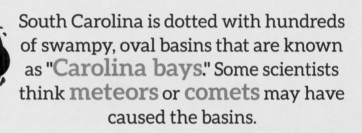

South Carolina is dotted with hundreds of swampy, oval basins that are known as "Carolina bays." Some scientists think meteors or comets may have caused the basins.

Sumter, South Carolina, has the largest **gingko farm** in the entire world.

The **Boykin Spaniel,** the official state dog of South Carolina, was first bred in the state as a hunting dog.

Brain Teasers

What have you learned about South Carolina after reading this book? Test your knowledge by answering these questions. All of the information can be found in the text you just read. The answers are provided below for easy reference.

1 What is the capital of South Carolina?

2 What two important American Revolutionary War victories did the colonists win in South Carolina?

3 What year did South Carolina secede from the Union and join the Confederate States of America?

4 What are South Carolina's three distinct land regions?

5 How much of South Carolina is forested?

6 What is one of South Carolina's leading agricultural products?

7 What explorer, in 1521, was the first to sail the coast of what is now South Carolina?

8 When was South Carolina split from North Carolina?

Key Words

erosion: the wearing away of rock and soil

improvisation: a performance done without previous preparation

justice: a judge in a court of law

parasailing: the sport of soaring in the air while harnessed to a parachute that is attached to a moving motorboat

patents: exclusive rights granted to inventors or companies to manufacture and sell their inventions

persecution: the act of continually treating someone in a harmful or cruel way, or being treated that way, especially because of one's beliefs or one's heritage

plantations: large estates where crops are grown

rural: of, or living in, the country

secede: to formally withdraw

steeplechase: a horse race on a course with artificial ditches, fences, and other obstacles over which the horses must jump

urban: of, or living in, the city

Index

Log on to www.av2books.com

AV² by Weigl brings you media enhanced books that support active learning. Go to www.av2books.com, and enter the special code found on page 2 of this book. You will gain access to enriched and enhanced content that supplements and complements this book. Content includes video, audio, weblinks, quizzes, a slide show, and activities.

AV² Online Navigation

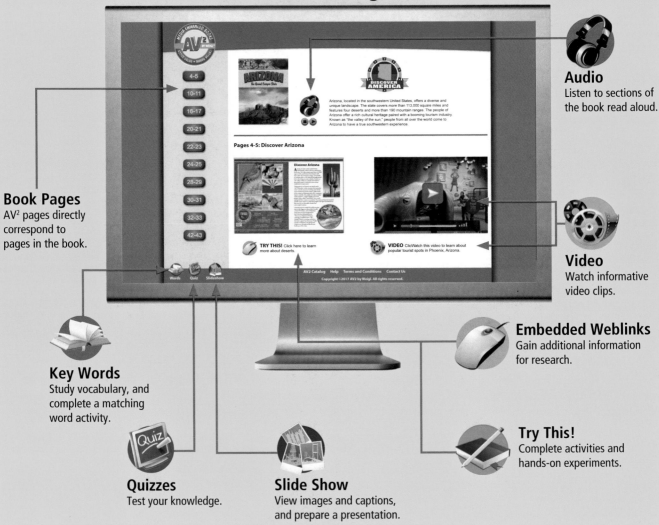

Book Pages
AV² pages directly correspond to pages in the book.

Audio
Listen to sections of the book read aloud.

Video
Watch informative video clips.

Key Words
Study vocabulary, and complete a matching word activity.

Embedded Weblinks
Gain additional information for research.

Quizzes
Test your knowledge.

Slide Show
View images and captions, and prepare a presentation.

Try This!
Complete activities and hands-on experiments.

AV² was built to bridge the gap between print and digital. We encourage you to tell us what you like and what you want to see in the future.

Sign up to be an AV² Ambassador at www.av2books.com/ambassador.